STEAMPUNK YOUR WARDROBE

STEAMPUNK YOUR WARDROBE

EASY PROJECTS TO ADD VICTORIAN FLAIR TO EVERYDAY FASHIONS

⟡ CALISTA TAYLOR ⟡

Design Originals

an Imprint of Fox Chapel Publishing

www.d-originals.com

ISBN: 978-1-57421-417-8

© 2012 by Design Originals, www.d-originals.com, an imprint of Fox Chapel Publishing 800-457-9112, 1970 Broad Street, East Petersburg, PA 17520.

Library of Congress Cataloging-in-Publication Data

Taylor, Calista.
  Steampunk your wardrobe / Calista Taylor.
    p. cm.
  ISBN 978-1-57421-417-8 (pbk.)
  1. Dress accessories. 2. Steampunk culture. I. Title.
TT649.8.T39 2012
391.4'4--dc23
                              2012007835

Printed in China

First Printing

DEDICATION

I would like to dedicate this book to my husband and girls for putting up with me as I took over the house with my projects. I would also like to thank my family and my critique partners for their endless support.

ACKNOWLEDGMENTS

I would like to thank Sierra Gitlin for being such a wonderful model and the Charles River Museum of Industry for allowing us to shoot photographs there.

ABOUT THE AUTHOR

Calista Taylor is an author of steampunk/gaslight romances and non-fiction craft books, and also works as a book cover designer. She resides in New England with her husband, her two girls, an ancient cat, and a crazy dog.

When not running things over with a sewing machine or lacing herself into a corset, Calista can be found tapping away on her laptop, tormenting her characters, and riddling the streets of Victorian London with dead bodies and heaving bosoms. She's also a creative cook who can't follow recipes, a versatile crafter, and a happy geek.

Above: Lace-edged Pantaloons, page 46

Facing Page: Victorian Lace Shirt, page 82; Hiked-up Skirt, page 44; Brown Capelet, page 92; Knit Bolero, page 62; Steampunk Charm Necklace, page 24

INSIDE YOU'LL LEARN ABOUT...

...producing cabbage rose embellishments, page 20.

...creating flawless ruffles, page 18.

...taking proper measurements, page 15.

...the origins of Steampunk, page 10

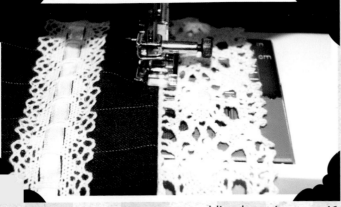

...adding lace trim, page 46.

...creating basic accessories, page 22.

...working with chains, page 24.

...bustling a skirt, page 50.

...making invisible stitches in lace, page 32.

...adding a lining to a bag, page 76.

...crafting simple clothing designs, page 42.

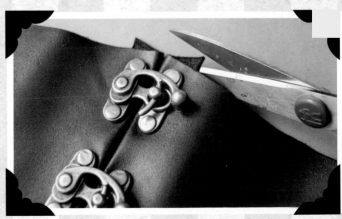

...working with leather, page 86.

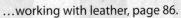
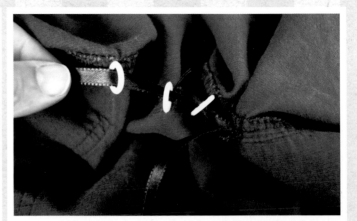

An Introduction to Steampunk

Though the term *steampunk* did not exist until the 1980s, the mix of Victoriana and fictional technological inventions that are prominent elements of the style first appeared in the writings of Jules Verne, Mary Shelley, and H. G. Wells.

Steampunk evolved into a subgenre of speculative science fiction that usually takes place during the Victorian era or in a world where Victorian aesthetics and ideologies are dominant. Always present are technological advances—often steam driven—that did not necessarily exist during the story's time period. While these fictional devices may be far more advanced than even our current technologies, they are always in keeping with the aesthetics of the story's setting. The technology is often used to better the lives of the characters and erase the inequalities of society that were so dominant during that time period.

Today, steampunk extends well beyond a genre of fiction. Its unique aesthetic can be found in clothing, jewelry, art, and everyday household items, often combining a Victorian feel with a modern twist, but always open to interpretation. As a result, steampunk is quite adaptable and flexible—from something Victorian in a traditional sense to something that has more of a post-apocalyptic feeling, as if a modern society has returned to the ways of old.

Often there's a re-appropriation of items, which can reflect the ingenuity found in the genre and aesthetic. A modern suit jacket can be gathered in the back and embellished with lace. A long skirt can be gathered, bustled, and hitched. Plastic welder's goggles can be altered and painted so they resemble the goggles of an airship captain. Sometimes, it is as simple as adorning an existing article with steampunk elements. Whether projects are original or created through alteration,

Feather Fascinator, page 28

Plum Shirt, page 96

there is no right or wrong. This makes it easy for novice and expert alike to participate in this fascinating and expanding culture.

Steampunk has seen such growth in recent years that it is often present in mainstream society, though people may not realize that an object is indeed steampunk or steampunk-inspired. From fashion, jewelry, and accessories that have taken on a modern Victorian feel, to recent movies such as *Sherlock Holmes*, *Alice in Wonderland*, and *Hugo*, steampunk can be found almost anywhere. With steampunk conventions popping up across this country and in other parts of the world, it is clear steampunk is a movement that is growing by leaps and bounds.

Though it is easy to create a head to toe steampunk outfit for a special event, adding individual pieces to a traditional wardrobe creates a unique flair that will still feel current and can be worn day to day. Also, since many items are repurposed, it is a great and inexpensive way to update out-of-style pieces and invigorate a wardrobe.

In addition to projects that repurpose already made clothing items, this book includes easy to make original items. Common elements of steampunk clothing are ruffles, pleats, lace, antiqued metals, leather, gears, airships, watch parts, octopi, and sparrows. Though there's usually a Victorian feel, steampunk also includes clothing with a safari, military, or aeronautical feel, harkening to the Victorian period's explorations and military ventures.

The best part of steampunk is that it is open to interpretation. So find your adventurous side, throw caution to the wind, and create your own style and version of steampunk.

Steampunk Charm Necklace, page 24
Leather Waist Cincher, Page 86

ABOUT THIS BOOK

Though steampunk fashion can often be taken to an extreme, the projects in this book are intended to introduce steampunk into your wardrobe by incorporating steampunk-inspired items. While some projects are made from scratch, most repurpose existing items, allowing you to breathe new life into objects you may have hidden away in your closet. Please feel free to use these instructions as a starting point, then add your own flair so you can make each creation truly your own. There are no rules when it comes to steampunk, so I hope you'll have fun with it.

GETTING STARTED

When looking for clothing to repurpose, start with your own closet. Clothing that never gets worn or has gone out of style is usually perfect for repurposing. If you cannot bring yourself to cut up or alter an expensive article of clothing, check local thrift stores, yard sales, and secondhand clothing or consignment shops. Most of the repurposed articles of clothing in this book came from the local church rummage sale or flea market.

For best results, choose items that already lean toward a Victorian aesthetic. Double-breasted, military-styled coats, long full skirts, and garments with puffy shoulders, fitted waists, or waists that cinch are all easily converted to steampunk style. When it comes to color, steampunk tends to use a lot of earth tones, particularly shades of brown. If the fabric has a pattern, it tends to be traditional. As a result, it is best to avoid modern or trendy colors and prints. Many steampunk elements can be found not only in the jewelry section of a craft store, but also in the scrapbooking section, and even the hardware store. Fabric and craft stores are also excellent resources, as are online stores and websites, such as the supply section of *www.Etsy.com*.

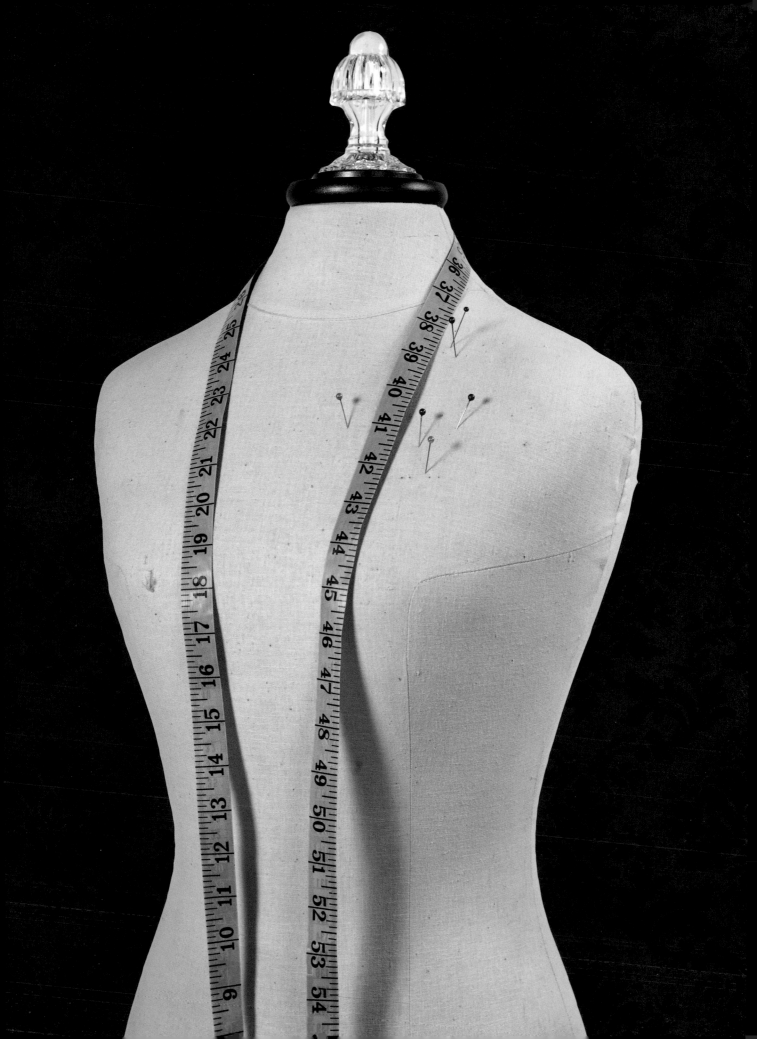

STEAMPUNK FASHION INSPIRATION

Take a look at what's possible when a fashion designer executes full-fledged steampunk fashion. These photos, excerpted from *Steampunk Fashion* by Evelyn Kriete, should inspire you to new levels. Start with the book in your hands and who knows what you'll come up with!

Designer: Twin Bee Design; Photographer: Anna Fischer; Model: Alexandra Abene

Designer: Topsy Turvy Design; Photographer: Silent Shudder Photography; Model: Beaux Deadly

Photographer: Tyrus Flynn; Model: Kat

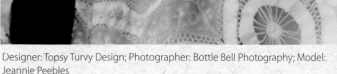

Designer: Topsy Turvy Design; Photographer: Bottle Bell Photography; Model: Jeannie Peebles

TAKING YOUR MEASUREMENTS

To assure that you are taking accurate measurements, stand in front of a full-length mirror and ue a flexible measuring tape. Before you record the measurement you're taking, check all sides and make sure that the tape is in the correct spot and didn't shift. Don't hold the tape too tightly or too loosely, it should be comfortably snug.

1 Bust measurement. Measure your bust across its fullest part. The measuring tape should continue across your back following where the strap of your bra would be.

2 Waist Measurement. Your waist measurement should be taken at the smallest part of your waist. Hold the tape comfortably in front and check the back before recording.

3 Hip Measurement. Similar to measuring your bust, your hip measurement should be taken across the fullest part. This should also include the fullest part of your rear as well. You may need to maneuver the tape to ensure that you are measuring the correct spot. Double check that the tape is placed evenly across the back and record the measurement.

TOOLS AND SUPPLIES

Just as your wardrobe can be a rich source of raw materials for steampunk projects, the home toolbox or workbench has nearly everything needed to complete the projects in this book. For those few exceptions, visit your local fabric or craft supply store.

Sewing machine—The projects in this book are designed to be completed by someone possessing only basic sewing skills. Still, a sewing machine will help to complete most of the repurposed clothing projects with ease. A ruffler sewing foot is a great addition, though ruffling fabric by hand works just as well.

Scissors and craft knife—A sharp pair of scissors is indispensable for cutting fabric with precision. To keep scissors sharp, only use them to cut fabric. A heavy-duty pair of shears, such as kitchen shears, is useful for cutting through leather. Also, a sharp utility or craft knife will come in handy.

Hot glue gun—A low-temperature glue gun is sufficient. Always follow the manufacturer's instructions for safe use and make sure the glue sticks used match the temperature of the glue gun. Keep a bowl of ice water close at hand when using.

Jewelry pliers—Needle-nose pliers, round-tip pliers, and wire cutters should be all you need. Jewelry-making kits containing all three items can often be purchased on a budget.

Adhesives—Some projects require a craft glue and a heavy duty adhesive, such as one used for jewelry making.

Hammer—A basic utilitarian hammer will work fine for setting rivets and grommets.

Leather hole punch—While some grommet and rivet sets come with hole punches, they might not be shar enough to cut through leather. A leat hole punch, either the kind with a ha or one that uses a hammer, will make the job easier, especially when it con to making a larger hole. For the sma holes, a sharp craft knife or a nail an hammer can be used.

A Few Things Before You Start

Here are some basic elements you will come across time and again in this book. As you will find, everything is open to interpretation, so find what works best for you. Don't be scared to experiment.

RUFFLES

Steampunk and Victorian clothing often feature ruffles. Here are three different techniques for creating ruffles. Experiment to find the one that is easiest and creates the desired look.

USING A RUFFLER FOOT

A ruffler foot is a sewing machine attachment that automatically gathers fabric into a ruffle. This attachment also will pleat one fabric while sewing it to a separate piece of fabric that remains flat. By adjusting the settings on the foot, you can change the depth and amount of ruffles per inch. Some fabrics work better than others with a ruffler foot, especially when trying to ruffle the edges of a folded piece of fabric. When using a ruffler, make sure to go at a slow speed and test a swatch of fabric first to see how compatible it is with the ruffler.

Although the ruffler is only intended to gather or pleat fabric along its edge, some models can be modified to permit gathering or pleating a piece of fabric down its middle. To do so, unscrew and remove the piece that keeps the fabric from feeding through the machine past its edge. It is located on the far right of the ruffler. Removing this piece will allow a piece of fabric to travel through the ruffler so that it is gathered or pleated down the middle rather than at the edge. This piece can easily be replaced to enable the ruffler to function as designed.

Rufflers can be set to make a ruffle every one, six, or twelve stitches. Which setting to use and how much extra fabric will be needed to create the ruffle depends upon how full a ruffle is desired. To calculate how long the fabric used to make the ruffle must be, first measure the length of the area that will

receive the ruffle. If more than one row of ruffles is desired, or if ruffles will be added to multiple places on a garment, add these lengths together then multiply the total as follows: For an extremely full ruffle, use setting 1 and multiply the total length by 4 or 5.

For a full ruffle, which is usually the standard for most projects, use setting 6 and multiply the total length by at least 2. For a slight ruffle, use setting 12 and multiply the total length by 1.25. It may be necessary to sew together multiple pieces in order to get a piece of fabric long enough to make the desired ruffle.

USING A RUNNING STITCH

Another way to create a ruffle is with a running stitch. If sewing by hand, thread a needle and knot the thread. Starting at one end of the ruffle fabric, insert the needle through the top of the fabric to the back side, and then bring it back up to the top. Draw the thread through the fabric, making a short stitch. Continue weaving the needle through the fabric, taking care to make the stitches the same size. How long each stitch is depends upon the type of ruffle desired. Longer stitches will produce deeper ruffles, while ruffles produced by shorter stitches are less full. Continue stitching across the entire

length of fabric from end to end, and then carefully push the fabric down the length of the thread. Once the ruffles are evenly spaced, knot the gathering thread. Use a sewing machine to sew a straight stitch through the gathering thread along the length of the gathered fabric to keep the ruffles in place. If desired, remove the original thread.

Ruffles can also be made on a sewing machine using a straight stitch. Adjust the stitch length to the maximum setting and loosen the upper tension slightly. Sew along the entire edge of the ruffle fabric then gently pull on the thread to create the ruffle.

FREEHAND RUFFLES

Another option is to gather the ruffle fabric as it is being sewn onto the garment. This can sometimes be a little tricky, and takes some getting used to, but once mastered, it is by far the quickest and easiest. Using a straight stitch, simply gather the fabric as it gets fed under the presser foot of the sewing machine. Try to maintain the density of the ruffles for an even look. Also, be generous when estimating the amount of fabric needed for the ruffle to avoid running out of fabric.

The advantage to this method is that it is quick and usually results in the fullest ruffles of all three techniques.

Cabbage Roses

A great embellishment, these roses can often be made of scrap fabric in different sizes and clustered together on a garment. Thin, lightweight fabrics, like lining or an iridescent sheer, work best. Before starting this project, please review the fire safety precautions below. Also, be careful to not hold the fabric stationary, since that can cause it to catch on fire. Finally, holding the fabric with tweezers can help keep you from burning your fingers, especially with the smaller pieces.

MATERIALS AND TOOLS

❏ 2 OR 3 COORDINATING SCRAPS OF SYNTHETIC FABRIC

❏ BEADS AND/OR PEARLS

❏ MATCHING THREAD

❏ FEATHERS (OPTIONAL)

❏ NEEDLE

❏ TWEEZERS

❏ TEA LIGHT CANDLE

A Word of Caution

Several projects in this book call for singeing the edges of fabric. Proper fire safety precautions should be taken when working with an open flame and flammable materials. A fire extinguisher should be readily at hand. Also make sure to work on a non-flammable surface and in a well-ventilated area. Test each fabric to get a feel for how flammable it is and how it will react. Only synthetic fabrics should be used because natural fibers will not melt for the desired effect, and can easily catch on fire.

1 **Cut out the flower circles.** Cut out between 7–10 circles for each flower, gradually decreasing the size of the circles. The largest circle should be approximately ⅛" (3mm) larger than the desired size of the finished flower. The shape and size of the circles do not need to be exact.

2 **Singe the edges.** With caution, hold the edge of the fabric 3–4" (75mm–100mm) over the tea candle's flame. Slowly move the fabric closer to the candle until the heat from the flame begins to melt the edge. Move the circle around to completely singe the edge.

3 **Curl the edges.** As the edge of the fabric melts, the circle may start to curl in. This is a desired effect because it will mimic the natural curve of a flower petal. If the fabric isn't naturally curling, move the underside of the fabric, near the edge, closer to the flame—this will cause it to curl away from the flame.

4 **Layer the circles.** Layer the singed circles on top of one another. Make sure the largest is on the bottom and the smallest on the top, with the other circles arranged in decreasing size. Also make sure the circles are curving up rather than under.

5 **Add beads.** Insert the threaded needle through the center of all of the layers, starting with the largest circle at the bottom and ending at the smallest circle on top. Thread a bead or pearl onto the needle, then pass it back through the layers, going from top to bottom. Repeat at least three times, adding as many beads as desired.

Easy Basics

Accessories can take an ordinary outfit and add the character needed to bring it to a new level. Steampunk accessories, especially, can add a unique Victorian flair to your wardrobe. The easy no-sew (or almost no-sew) accessory projects in this chapter are a good starting point for those just entering the world of steampunk fashion. And, because they are accessories, these projects can be paired with any item in your closet—a suit, a dress, a casual daytime outfit—the possibilities are endless! In addition, you can customize each piece to fit your personal taste by selecting different materials than those listed. So have fun, experiment, and accessorize!

STEAMPUNK CHARM NECKLACE

Used in combination with the right components, a simple chain can be transformed into a Steampunk Charm Necklace. The metal chain gives the piece an edgy look, while the filigree on the pendant adds a touch of Victorian style. Add more chain to make the necklace longer, or alter the design by adding extra charms, pearls, or beads. It's the perfect way to add a subtle hint of steampunk flair to any outfit.

MATERIALS AND TOOLS

- ❑ Chain (at least 24" (610mm) total, more if a longer necklace is desired)
- ❑ Filigree pendant
- ❑ Jump rings
- ❑ Various charms, pearls, or beads
- ❑ 2 nuts (gears or small filigree pieces will also work)
- ❑ Necklace clasp
- ❑ 2 Jewelry pliers
- ❑ Bead reamer

1 **Cut the chains.** Cut 2 lengths of chain approximately 4" (100mm) long, and then another 2 lengths of chain approximately 4¾" (120mm) long. If desired, different types of chain may be used, as is the case in our example. This will give the necklace more visual interest, though it is not necessary.

2 **Attach the jump ring.** Open a jump ring and string one of the short lengths of chain, then a long one, followed by the pendant, and then a long length of chain and lastly, a short length of chain. Close the jump ring. The necklace will have mirror images of the chains, with the pendant in the middle.

3 **Attach the charm.** Using another jump ring, attach a charm to the bottom of the filigree pendant. If necessary, enlarge the hole in the filigree with a bead reamer or the nose of a very thin, round-tipped jewelry plier.

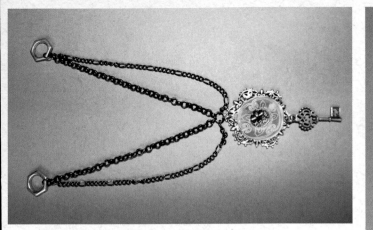

4 **Join the chains.** Join the two lengths of chain on each side of the pendant. Add a nut, gear, or filigree piece before closing the jump ring.

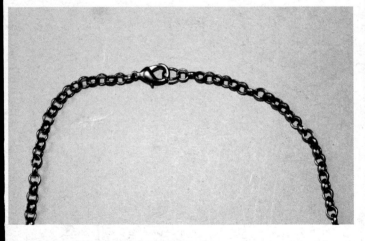

5 **Attach the clasp.** Cut 2 lengths of chain each approximately 3¼" (85mm) long. If a longer necklace is desired, make these pieces of chain longer. Attach one length of chain to each nut. On the free ends of those two chains, attach the necklace clasp.

6 **Add some embellishments.** Embellish the necklace with charms, pearls, and beads. Use jump rings to attach the embellishments.

Feather Fascinator

A feather fascinator is a great accessory that works with both long and short hair. Use it as a barrette to hold hair at the back of your head, or make a dramatic statement by placing it close to your face. You can even replace the hair clip with a pin back and wear it on a jacket or shirt. There are hundreds of feather types and colors available, so use your creativity to make this feather fascinator truly your own. For the largest variety of feathers, visit millinery suppliers near you or check out *www.Etsy.com* under supplies.

MATERIALS AND TOOLS

- ❏ Feathers

- ❏ Small piece of felt—a 2" x 2" (50 x 50mm) square should be sufficient—in a coordinating color

- ❏ Craft glue

- ❏ A small brooch, pendant, or bejeweled button

- ❏ A small alligator-type hair clip

- ❏ Hot glue gun (preferably low temp)

- ❏ Craft knife

- ❏ Scissors

- ❏ Toothpick

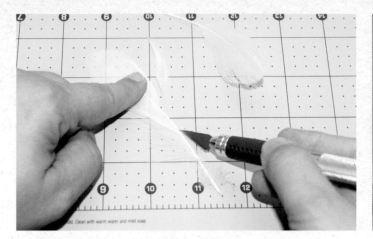

1 **Trim the Feathers.** Choose a variety of feathers that complement each other. The project shown uses ostrich, goose, and peacock feathers, but feel free to experiment with other types. Using a craft knife or scissors, trim the feathers to the desired size and shape. Keep all feather scraps since they may be useful in other projects.

2 **Curl desired feathers.** If desired, curl the feathers using the same method used to curl ribbon, running the shaft or surface barbs up against a scissor edge or the back end of a knife.

3 **Gather and glue small feathers.** Gather small or single-strand feathers or barbs and glue them together with the craft glue. Set aside and wait until glue is dry. Cut the felt into a circle or teardrop shape. This will serve as the base for the feathers.

4 **Arrange and attach the feathers to the felt.**
Arrange the feathers on the felt in a pleasing composition. Starting at the back, apply a small amount of hot glue to the bottom underside of the feathers and glue into place on the felt. Continue adding feathers until all are attached to the felt. Trim any extra felt that is visible, taking care to not cut the feathers.

5 **Attach the embellishment.** Finish the front by gluing on the pendant, button, or brooch. The embellishment should lay relatively flat atop the feathers, so remove anything from its back before attaching it.

6 **Attach the alligator clip.** Glue or sew the alligator clip on the underside. Although hot glue will work, epoxy glue will be more durable. If desired, also glue a pin next to the alligator clip so the fascinator can double as a brooch.

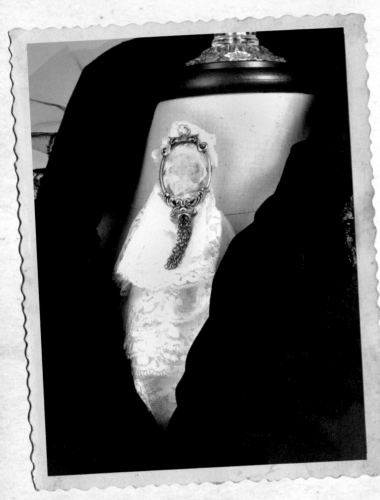

LACE BROOCH NECK RUFF

This project is the perfect accent for a traditional shirt or blouse, making it the perfect way to bring steampunk to work. Or, wear it with something completely unexpected for a unique, Victorian touch. If you want to add a pop of color to an outfit, try dying the lace to achieve the desired effect. This lacy piece also makes a great handbag accessory.

MATERIALS

- ❑ 18" (455MM) SQUARE OF CHEESECLOTH OR A VERY THIN GAUZE

- ❑ 1 YD. (1M) 3" (75MM)-WIDE LACE

- ❑ MATCHING LACE

- ❑ 1 BROOCH, PENDANT, OR LARGE INTRICATE BUTTON

- ❑ 1 PIN BACK

1 **Fold and gather the cheesecloth.** Fold the square of cheesecloth in half and then loosely gather it at the fold, pinching it together. Lay it down so that the fold is at the top and the open end of fabric is at the bottom. Stitch in place at the top near the fold.

2 **Zigzag-fold the lace.** Fold the lace in a zigzag pattern, slightly offsetting each layer so that the scalloped edge from each fold is visible. The zigzags should be approximately 3" (75mm) wide at the bottom and gradually narrow to approximately 2" (50mm) at the very top.

3 **Invisibly stitch the lace folds.** Turn the lace over and stitch the folds in place, taking care to make sure the stitches are not visible and that the front folds of lace are still free. This is most easily done by using the outer most fold of lace to mask your stitch in the layer below it.

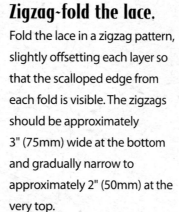

4 **Sew together the lace and cheesecloth.** Lay the lace on top of the cheesecloth, matching the narrow end of the lace with the gathered and folded edge of the cheesecloth. Sew across the top, leaving the bottom of the lace and cheesecloth free.

5 **Attach the brooch.** Securely sew the brooch or pendant to the top of the lace. Sew the pin back to the top of the cheesecloth, behind where the brooch is located.

RUFFLED LACE CHOKER

A wide choker like this one makes a bold statement. Customize the design by using a favorite brooch or adding different types of feathers. You can also experiment with different colors of ribbon and lace. If you want a less dramatic look, decrease the width of the choker, or leave the lace out entirely and craft the piece using ribbon, a brooch, and feathers.

MATERIALS AND TOOLS

- ❑ 1 YD. (1M) 2" (50MM)-WIDE LACE, SCALLOPED ON ONE SIDE

- ❑ ½ YD. (455MM) ½" (15MM) PLEATED TRIM

- ❑ ½ YD. (455MM) ½"–¾" (15MM–20MM) OPAQUE TRIM

- ❑ NECKLACE CLASP FOR WIDE RIBBON NECKLACE

- ❑ LARGE BROOCH, CAMEO, OR FILIGREE

- ❑ FEATHERS (OPTIONAL)

- ❑ HOT GLUE GUN OR FABRIC GLUE

- ❑ HEAVY-DUTY GLUE

- ❑ PLIERS

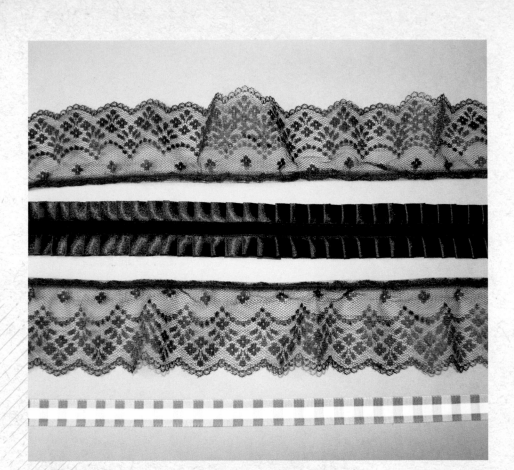

1 Measure your neck and cut fabric.

Measure the circumference of your neck. Do not add any ease. Using this measurement, cut 2 pieces of the lace and 1 piece each of the two trims. If the trims are made of a synthetic fabric, carefully singe their edges to prevent fraying. Lace usually does not fray, so it is unnecessary to singe its edges.

2 Attach the lace to the trim.

Lay the pleated trim right side down. Using hot glue or fabric glue, attach the long straight edge of one piece of lace to the center back of the pleated trim. Repeat on the opposite side of the trim with the second piece of lace.

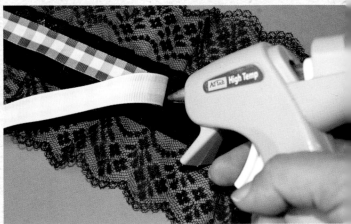

3 Glue on the backing trim.

Glue the opaque trim to the wrong side of the pleated trim, covering the straight edges of the lace.

4 **Attach the clasp.** Place a drop of glue on the inside of one section of the ribbon clasp. Center the open end of the clasp on the short edge of ruffled trim and crimp to hold in place. Repeat on the opposite end of choker with the other piece of the ribbon clasp.

5 **Make and add the embellishment.** If desired, glue feathers to the back of the brooch with craft glue. Leave a small area in the center of the broach uncovered. Glue the embellishment to the front center of the choker.

EMBELLISHED FLASK

You might not want to carry a flask with you everywhere you go, but this piece makes a great addition to a costume for a party. You can also use it as a decoration in your home—it will certainly be a great conversation starter! In addition to paper, fabric and leather also work well with this project. You can select an alternative focal image for your flask, like a set of gears, an image of Victorian London, or a photo of a Victorian lady.

MATERIALS

- ❑ Metal flask (new or old)

- ❑ Decorative scrapbook paper, fabric, or leather (large enough to encircle the flask)

- ❑ 1 yd. (1m) narrow trim

- ❑ Coordinating papers and/or images (optional)

- ❑ Metallic acrylic craft paint (optional)

- ❑ Metal scrapbook embellishments, such as frames, corners, and/or gears (optional)

- ❑ Craft glue or other adhesive appropriate for covering material

- ❑ Heavy-duty glue

1 **Measure out the paper.** Wrap the body of the flask with the scrapbook paper, allowing for a slight overlap, and mark how much is needed. Also mark the height of the body of the flask. Cut the material to size.

2 **Adhere the paper.** Cover the body of the flask with a thin layer of craft glue or other appropriate adhesive. Apply the paper, taking care to glue down the seam. Let the glue dry. Attach any images or paper embellishments with glue, leaving space at the top and bottom edges for trim.

3 **Brush on metallic paint.** Next, you will add metallic paint to make the paper look aged and interesting. Test the paint on a scrap of paper first and thin, if necessary, to achieve the desired effect. Brush a thin layer of paint on the paper and any images that have been glued to the flask. Blot with a paper towel for a more transparent effect. If desired, apply decoupage glue to the surface of the paper for additional protection.

4 **Place the embellishments.** Determine the placement of metal embellishments. If necessary, gently bend them so they lay flat against the flask. If desired, paint the embellishments.

5 **Attach the embellishments.** Attach the metal embellishments to the flask with the heavy-duty glue. If using a frame, images may be inserted prior to gluing it to the flask.

6 **Apply the trim.** Using craft glue, apply trim to the top and bottom of edges of the flask body, covering the edge of the paper. Fold under the raw edge of the trim and glue to the flask.

CHAPTER

3

Easy Clothing Projects

When repurposing clothing, it is not necessary to duplicate the exact style of clothing shown in this book. Anything similar should work, even with some minor adjustments to the instructions. Remember, make the clothing your own—anything goes with steampunk. Just keep in mind the various aesthetics that make the genre what it is. It often takes no more than minor embellishments with lace or ruffles, the addition of some cogs, chains, or corseting, or adding a gathered waist or bustle to achieve the desired aesthetic.

Hiked-up Skirt

Just a few embellishments take an ordinary skirt and give it a bohemian, steampunk flair. For a more dramatic look, layer this skirt over another long, full skirt. Alter the embellishments by using chain and attach charms instead of a beaded necklace as shown.

Students of John Mickelson, head of the Wentworth Institute of Technology's Pattern Making Department from 1911 to 1947, constructed the wooden model that serves as the backdrop for this photo. The piece is a quarter-scale Walschaerts Locomotive Valve Gear model, based on a 4-6-2 Pacific Type steam locomotive of the American Locomotive Company of Schenectady, New York. The model uses mahogany for cast iron parts and maple for cast steel parts. It employs an early radial valve gear created by Egide Walschaerts, a Belgian railway mechanical engineer. Unlike the earlier Stephenson gear, the Walschaerts gear could be serviced without an inspection and repair pit.

MATERIALS

- ❏ 1 FULL SKIRT, CALF TO ANKLE LENGTH

- ❏ MATCHING THREAD

- ❏ 3–4 CLASPS OR HOOKS

- ❏ 3–4 JUMP RINGS OR D-RINGS

- ❏ CHAIN AND BEADS, OR NECKLACES

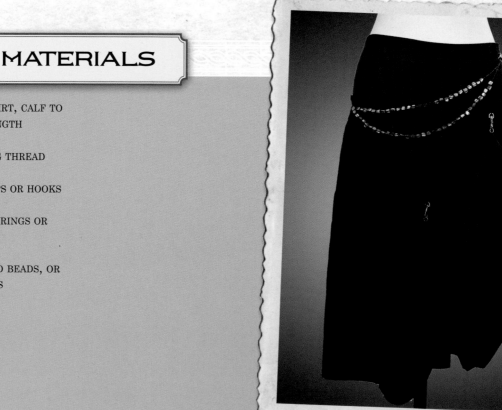

1 **Determine the clasp placement.** Mark a spot just to the front of the side seam and about 9" (230mm) from the hem of the skirt. On the same side of the skirt, mark a second spot about 12" (305mm) down from the waist. Pin these two spots together to see how the final skirt will look. If necessary, adjust the position of either mark to create the desired look.

2 **Sew on the jump ring and clasps.** Sew the clasp or hook to the skirt at the spot below the waist. Sew a jump ring to the spot marked just above the hem. Join the jump ring to the clasp or hook.

3 **Create a second hike.** If desired, mark a second location to hike up the skirt and attach another clasp or hook and jump ring.

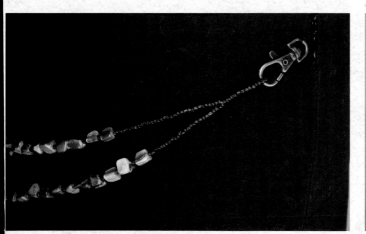

4 **Attach the chain or necklace.** To attach the chain or necklace, mark a spot on the side of the skirt below the waist but above the original 12" (305mm) mark. Mark a second spot on the opposite side of the skirt at the waist. Pin one end of the chain or necklace to each of these spots. If necessary, adjust the position of either spot to achieve the desired look. Sew a clasp on the spot below the waist and a jump ring on the spot at the waist.

5 **Attach more chains and beads if desired.** Adorn the waist area with multiple chains and beads, stringing them between the clasp and the ring. Note: Long multi-strand necklaces are an easy way to achieve this look.

LACE-EDGED PANTALOONS

Ribbon and lace will turn the most business-like pants into something fun and flirty. The shortened length is a modern twist on Victorian pantaloons and makes these a great piece for your summer wardrobe. Use colored ribbon for a subtle design alteration, or try adding black lace and ribbon to a black pair of tailored pants.

Wearing Lace-edged Pantaloons and a Victorian-style blouse, model Sierra Gitlin fits right in with this Victorian fire engine. The vehicle is a Waltham Steam-Pumper Fire Engine 1, Waltham's first powered fire-fighting vehicle. Drawn by a team of four horses, the engine was in service from 1871 until the 1930s.

MATERIALS

- ❑ 1 PAIR TAILORED PANTS

- ❑ 1½ YD. (1½M) LACE TRIM WITH RIBBON WOVEN THROUGH THE CENTER

- ❑ 1½ YD. (1½M) LACE EDGING

- ❑ MATCHING THREAD

- ❑ SEAM SEALANT

1 **Measure and cut pants.** Choose a pair of pants with a wide, straight leg. Measure from your waist to the bend of your knee, and then add 4" (100mm) to that length. This total is the length of the side seam. From the waistband of the pants, measure this length down each side seam and make a mark. Cut the pant legs at that mark.

2 **Pin on the lace trim.** Pin the lace trim to the pant leg 2" (50mm) from the bottom and starting at the lower outside edge of the side seam. Leave 1" (25mm) at each end of the trim. Remove the ribbon from the extra trim and fold under ½" (15mm) of the trim. Repeat for second pant leg.

3 **Sew on the lace trim.** Sew the trim to the pant leg using two rows of straight stitching, one on each side of the lace near the ribbon. Take care not to sew through the ribbon because it must be free to be pulled into a gather.

4 **Sew on the lace edging.** Pin the straight edge of the lace edging to the raw edge of the pant leg. Start at the inseam and match right sides. Leave an extra ½" (15mm) at each end of the trim. Sew with a straight stitch. Matching right sides and using a ½" (15mm) seam, sew the ends of the edging together.

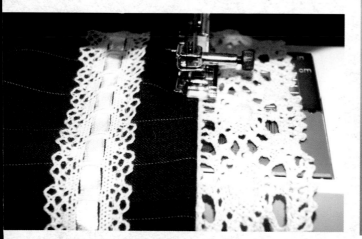

5 **Stitch the hem.** Turn up the hem, bringing the lace down to the edge of the pant leg and tucking under the raw edge of the pant leg and lace. Stitch the hem in place with a straight stitch that runs parallel to the seam.

6 **Gather the ribbon in the lace trim.** Gather the pant leg by pulling on the ribbon that is woven through the lace trim. Tie in a bow. Use seam sealant on the cut edges of the ribbon to prevent fraying.

BUSTLED A-LINE SKIRT

This skirt can be bustled in different ways, producing different looks for various occasions. The skirt I used for this project is made of a heavy, thick fabric, which gives the bustle more volume. You can also bustle a skirt with a light, flowing fabric for an alternative look. If you're feeling extra adventurous, try using this design concept to create curtains for a room in your home. Then you'll have your own steampunk fashion studio!

The Mergenthaler Linotype creates a stunning background for this steampunk fashion shot. Invented in 1884 by Ottmar Mergenthaler, the linotype revolutionized typesetting. In fact, Thomas Edison called it the eighth wonder of the world. While earlier typesetting required an individual to set pre-cast letters, typically by hand, the linotype assembled lines of individual brass molds from which single lines of type were cast. The lines were combined into columns, which were then combined and sent to the printer to produce a magazine or newspaper. This particular machine was used in the City of Boston Print Shop.

MATERIALS

❑ 1 FULL OR A-LINE SKIRT, CALF TO ANKLE LENGTH

❑ MATCHING THREAD

❑ 12 ½" (15MM) PLASTIC RINGS

❑ 1 SPOOL ¼" (5MM)-WIDE SATIN RIBBON

❑ SEAM SEALANT

1 **Measure and mark the lines where the ribbons will be.** Turn the skirt inside out. Measure the front of the skirt between the two side seams at the waistline and again at the hem. Divide each measurement by four. At the waistline, measure from the side seam toward the front and make a mark at a distance equal to one-quarter the distance between side seams. At the hem, measure from the side seam toward the front of the skirt and make a mark equal to one-quarter the distance between the side seams. Draw a line down the skirt connecting these two points. Repeat on the opposite side of the front of the skirt and on the back of the skirt.

2 **Sew on the plastic rings for the front of the skirt.** On each line on the front of the skirt, make marks at 9" (230mm), 14" (355mm), 21" (535mm), and 31" (785mm) from the waistline. Stitch a plastic ring to the first three marks.

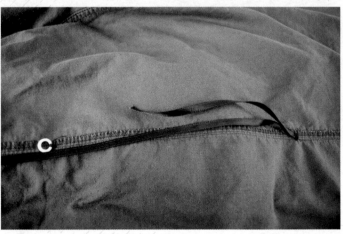

3 **Sew down the ribbons.** Cut five pieces of satin ribbon equal to the length of the skirt. Singe or seal the ends with seam sealant to prevent fraying. Fold the ribbon 6" (150mm) from one end, creating one very long piece with a short tail. Place the fold mark of the ribbon on the skirt at the mark without a ring and stitch. Repeat on the opposite side of the skirt front.

4 **Sew on the plastic rings and ribbons for the back lines of the skirt.** On the lines on the back of the skirt, make marks at 15" (380mm) and 25" (635mm) from the waistline. Stitch a plastic ring at the first mark and a folded piece of ribbon at the second mark.

5 **Sew on the plastic ring and ribbon on the center back seam.** On the center back seam, make marks at 9" (230mm) and 16" (405mm) from the waistline. Stitch a plastic ring at the first mark and then a folded piece of ribbon at the second mark.

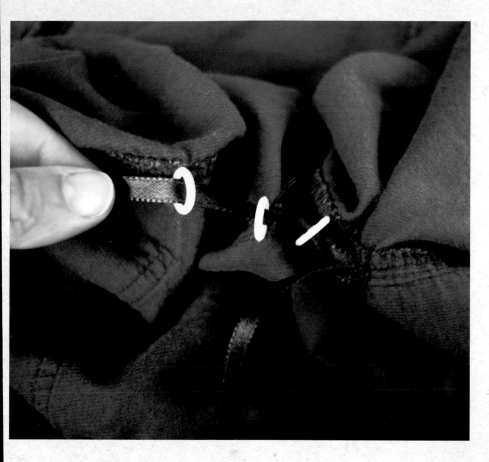

6 **Thread the rings**. To create the bustle, thread the long end of the ribbon up through each lace ring directly above it and tie in place using the short end. If necessary, trim the long end so it does not hang below the hiked up hem.

7 **Customize your skirt.** If desired, add more rings or pick and choose which rings to thread the ribbon through to create a different look. The ribbon can also be secured out of the way and the skirt worn long in its original form.

Lacy Circle Top

If you're looking for simple, this project is easy to make and even easier to wear. Make sure you select a soft, sheer, gauzy, or lacy fabric for the shirt, keeping in mind that you can choose fabrics in any color you desire. Mix hard and soft by cinching the shirt with a leather or chain belt instead of with a ribbon as shown.

MATERIALS

- ❏ 2–2½ YD. (2–2½ M)
  FABRIC

- ❏ 1 YD. (1M) 1–2½"
  (25–65MM) LACE

- ❏ 2 YD. (2M) ½" (15MM)
  RIBBON OR LACE

- ❏ MATCHING THREAD

1 Determine the length and width.

To determine the length, measure from your shoulder down past your waist to the point where you want the top to end. To determine the width, measure from the center of your sternum to the point on your arm where you want the sleeves to end.

2 Fold the material and pin it. Fold the fabric
in half lengthwise then again width wise and pin together. Pin the corner of the fold, so you can easily find the center again.

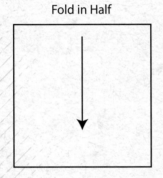

Fold in Half

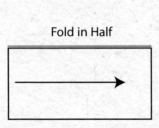

Fold in Half

Center

Folds are at the top and left

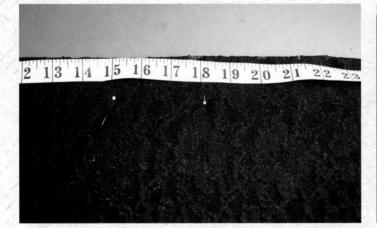

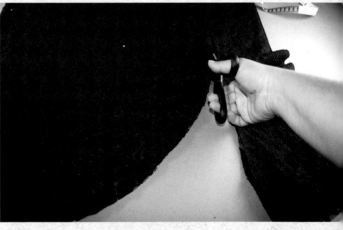

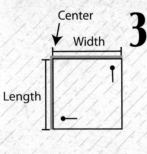

Center
Width
Length

3 Measure and mark the width and length on the fabric. Transfer
the length and width measurements calculated in step one to the folded fabric and mark with pins.

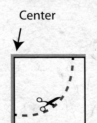

Center

4 Cut a curve connecting the points. Using a fabric
pencil or chalk, connect the marks with a sweeping arc so that it forms a quarter of a circl or oval. Pin the fabric together along the arc. Cut through all the layers of fabric, following the arc Finish the cut edge with a hem or zigzag stitch.

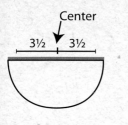

5 Mark the neck opening. Fold the fabric so that it is only folded in half at the shoulder. Make a mark 3½" (70mm) on either side of the center. Cut between the two marks to create a neck opening.

6 Create the neckline. While wearing the top, determine where the V-neck should end and mark with a pin. Carefully remove the top and make a mark ¼" (5mm) above the pin. Draw a line from this mark to the edges of the neck opening. Carefully cut along the line to create the front neckline.

7 Finish the neckline. To prevent stretching or fraying, finish the cut edge of the neckline with a zigzag stitch or bias tape.

8 Sew the neck trim. Pin the wide trim to the neckline, with the wrong side of the trim against the right side of the fabric. Miter the trim at the bottom of the V-neck. Stitch in place.

9 Mark the tie location. Measure from the top of the shoulder to the point between the bust and the waistline where the tie is desired. Transfer that measurement to the front and back of the shirt and make a horizontal mark with pins, chalk, or other temporary marker.

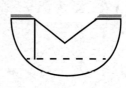

10 Measure the button hole locations. Measure the distance from the center front of the chest to just past the shoulder. Transfer that measurement to the lines made in step nine, measuring from both sides of the center front and back lines.

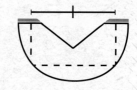

11 Cut the buttonholes. Make a small cut in the shirt at the marks made in step 9. For fabrics that ravel, sew a small buttonhole at each of the marks. Thread the narrow ribbon or lace through the holes, bringing both free ends to the front of the shirt. Tie with a bow.

SHOULDER WRAP

A ruffled shoulder wrap adds a splash of Victorian styling to any outfit. Instead of a traditional wrap or shrug, wear this piece with a dress for your next evening out—you're certain to spark some steampunk style envy. For best results, select a fabric with body that is still soft enough to gather, such as dupioni silk.

MATERIALS

- ❏ 1 YD. (1M) 54" (1½M)-WIDE FABRIC

- ❏ 1 YD. (1M) 2" (50MM)-WIDE COORDINATING OR MATCHING RIBBON, CUT IN HALF

- ❏ MATCHING THREAD

- ❏ FLOWERS, FEATHERS, JEWELS, OR LACE FOR EMBELLISHING

1 **Cut the fabric pieces.** Cut two pieces of fabric 16" (405mm) long and the full width of the fabric.

2 **Sew together along short side.** Matching right sides, sew the two pieces together along one of the short sides, creating one piece of fabric approximately 9 feet (3m) long. Press the seam open.

3 **Fold the fabric.** Fold the fabric in half lengthwise, right sides together, creating a piece approximately 9 feet (3m) long and 8 inches (203mm) wide. Match the edges and the center seam and pin. Stitch only along the long edge. Press seam open, taking care to not iron over the folded edges of the fabric.

4 **Sew down the middle.** Turn the fabric right side out. Line up the long seam with the center of the fabric so the seam runs right down the middle. Pin. Using a straight stitch, sew through both layers on the seam.

5 **Create the gathers.** Gather or pleat along the full length of the fabric. Use either a modified ruffling foot and a sewing machine or make the gathers or pleats by hand (see page 18).

6 **Measure the length the wrap should be.** Run a tape measure from the center of your back under one arm pit toward the chest, up behind the neck, back down the chest, and under the opposite arm pit to the starting point. Transfer this measurement to the ruffled fabric, placing the seam connecting the two lengths in the middle of the length, and cut.

7 **Attach the ribbon.** Pleat the fabric at one end of the wrap. Place one end of the ribbon in the middle of the pleats and fold the fabric edge over the ribbon twice. Pin in place and stitch, catching the ribbon in the folds of the pleated fabric. Repeat with a second piece of ribbon on the other end of the wrap.

8 **Attach some embellishments.** Embellish with flowers, pearls, feathers, chains, and/or ribbon. If desired, attach a clasp in the front to join the two sides. To wear, place the seam at the back of the neck, bring both ends over the shoulders toward the chest, then down under the arm pits and toward the back. Tie bow in back to keep the ribbon in place.

Knit Bolero

Steampunk styling comes easily with this bolero. It is the perfect piece to give any outfit a steampunk accent. For best results, start with a sweater that fits comfortably but is not too large. Remember, you can customize your look by selecting a sweater with a different color than the one shown. Or try trimming a dark-colored sweater with light-colored lace or a light-colored sweater with dark-colored lace.

MATERIALS

- [ ] 1 LIGHT-WEIGHT KNIT SWEATER

- [ ] 3 YD. (3M) RUFFLED LACE TRIM (ENOUGH TO GO ALL THE WAY AROUND THE BOLERO AND TO MAKE CAP SLEEVES)

- [ ] 3 BUTTONS OR SMALL BOWS

- [ ] SEAM SEALANT

- [ ] FABRIC MARKER

- [ ] EMBELLISHMENTS (SUCH AS PEARLS, BEADS, FEATHERS, AND FABRIC FLOWERS)

1 **Sew the armhole.** With a sewing machine, zigzag the body of the sweater just inside the armhole seam. Make sure to go completely around each armhole. This will help to keep the sweater from unraveling. If desired, apply seam sealant over the stitches for additional stability.

2 **Remove the sleeves.** Cut the sleeves off the sweater, leaving the armhole seam intact.

3 **Draw the first front cutting lines.** Draw a line down the front of the sweater. Begin at the shoulder seam approximately 3" (75mm) from the armhole and curve slightly toward the center to a point approximately even with the underarm seam. Curve the line down and around and continue to the side seam approximately 4" (100mm) below the underarm seam.

4 **Mark the remaining lines.** Mark a line on the opposite side of the sweater that is a mirror image of the first line. Take extra care to make sure both sides are even. Mark a line across the back of the sweater that connects the two lines on either side of the front.

5 **Zigzag stitch along the lines.** Run a zigzag stitch along the mark. Cut the sweater just outside the stitch, creating a bolero shape.

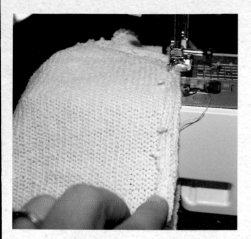

6 **Stitch the armholes edges.** Turn in the raw edges along the armholes and sew with a straight stitch.

7 **Sew on the lace trim.** Pin the straight edge of the lace trim to the edge of the sweater, right sides together and starting at one of the side seams. Sew with a straight stitch.

8 **Stitch the hem.** Turn under the raw edge of the sweater, bringing the lace trim to the right side edge of the sweater. Stitch hem in place using a straight stitch.

9 **Create the cap sleeves.** Cut two 7"–8" (180–205mm) pieces of the lace trim. Gather each cut edge so they come to a point. Stitch to secure the gathers. Fold the lace in half to find the midpoint. Pin the right side of the lace to the wrong side of the armholes, placing the midpoint at the shoulder seam. Stitch.

10 **Adjust the appearance.** If the sweater has stretched out in the back, creating an undesired flair, gather or pleat the extra fabric at the bottom in two or three evenly spaced locations, and tack in place. Embellish with a button or small bow to hide thread. Embellish the bolero as desired.

STEAMPUNK AHEAD!

You've learned how to make steampunk accessories and punch up your wardrobe with some great steampunk-inspired designs. Now it's time to take your steampunk styling to the next level with these standout pieces that are sure to impress. What's great about this chapter is that even though these projects are a bit more complicated than the previous ones, they are still quite easy to accomplish. There are a few extra steps involved, but nothing more than basic sewing skills are required. Pick a project and give it a try—you'll be amazed by the results!

Miniature Top Hat

This miniature top hat builds on the feather fascinator project from the second chapter to create a one-of-a-kind hairpiece. The design can easily be customized with different colors of fabric, ribbon, and embellishments. You can also alter this project to make place card holders for your next steampunk event. I recommend forming the hat out of cereal box cardboard, which has just the right amount of flexibility. For best results, use a synthetic fabric.

MATERIALS

- ❏ 1 LARGE CARDBOARD CEREAL BOX
- ❏ ¼ YD. (230MM) DECORATIVE FABRIC
- ❏ ⅓ YD. (305MM) OF 1" (25MM) TRIM
- ❏ ¾ YD. (685MM) FLEXIBLE TRIM APPROXIMATELY ¼" (5MM) WIDE
- ❏ TAPE

- ❏ FABRIC MARKER
- ❏ CRAFT GLUE
- ❏ HOT GLUE
- ❏ A VARIETY OF FEATHERS
- ❏ BROOCH OR BUTTON
- ❏ MEDIUM- TO LARGE-SIZE ALLIGATOR HAIR CLIP (WITH THE TEETH)

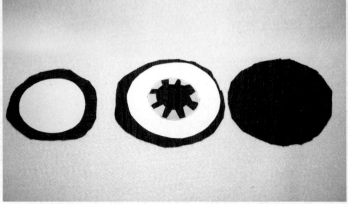

1 **Trace the pattern.** Using the template on page 102 as a guide, trace the pattern pieces onto a piece of cereal box cardboard, taking care to avoid any folds or creases in the box.

2 **Cut the cardboard pieces.** Cut out the pieces of cardboard and fold back the tabs.

3 **Cut out the top and brim fabric.** Place the top and brim pattern pieces on the fabric and trace with a pencil or fabric marker, adding ½" (15mm) seam allowance. Mark two pieces for the brim. Cut the fabric out along the lines. Using the template as a guide, mark and cut the center from one of the pieces of the brim fabric.

4 **Cut out the side band fabric.** Place the sideband pattern piece on the fabric and trace with a pencil or fabric marker. If using a synthetic fabric, add 1" (25 mm) to the length only. If using a natural fabric, add 1" to the length and ½" (15mm) to the width. Cut out. Do not cut out the tabs.

5 **Tape the sideband cylinder.** Bring the short edges of the sideband together and hold. Place the cylinder over the tabs on the brim and adjust the sideband so that the 2 pieces fit together. Secure the sideband with tape on both the inside and outside of the seam for stability.

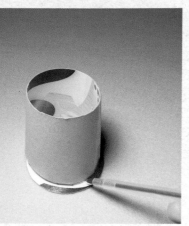

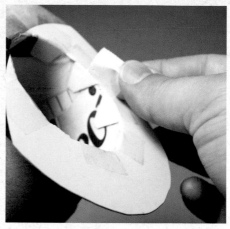

6 **Trim the top cardboard piece.** Place the larger end of the sideband upside down on the top template and trace. Trim any excess from the top.

7 **Tape the top and sideband cardboard.** Secure the top cardboard to the large end of the sideband with adhesive tape, taping both the inside and outside of the seam for stability.

8 **Tape on the brim.** Test the brim fabric with the center cuts over the sideband so it sits loose and out of the way. Fit the open end of the sideband over the tabs of the brim and tape the seams inside and out until secure.

9 **Glue the top fabric piece.** Apply a thin layer of fabric safe glue to the top of the hat. Center the top fabric over the glue and apply gentle pressure. With sharp scissors, clip the edges of the top fabric, forming tabs. Glue the tabs to the sideband, taking care to not get glue on the right side of the fabric.

10 **Glue on the brim fabric.** Move the brim fabric out of the way and apply a thin layer of glue to the brim cardboard. Carefully slide the oval down and apply gentle pressure. Add additional glue to the sideband to secure the tabs, taking care to not get glue on the right side of the fabric.

11 **Glue on the sideband fabric.** Determine the placement of the feathers. Apply a thin layer of glue to the sideband. Starting near the point where the feathers will be attached, place the sideband fabric on the glue. Take extra care to line up the edge of the fabric with the top of the hat. Make sure the fabric lies flat against the sides, especially at the bottom. Using a low-temperature glue gun, fold under the raw edge, and glue it into place against the hat.

12 **Glue on the underside brim fabric.** Apply a thin layer of glue to the underside of the top hat brim and gently press it against the wrong side of the brim fabric. Allow the glue to dry then trim the excess fabric from around the brim. Do not cut out the middle.

13 **Add trim to the brim.** Attach a thin piece of bias tape, trim, or thin flexible ribbon to the raw edge of the brim with fabric glue or a hot glue gun.

14 **Add some embellishments.** Embellish the hat as desired. The hat shown was decorated with feathers, ribbon, and a faceted gem. Tulle, gears, cameos, beads, and buttons may also be added.

15 **Sew on the alligator clip.** Sew an alligator hair clip to the underside of the brim, so that the hat can be securely worn. This step is best left for last because it is easier to determine ideal placement for the hat after it has been decorated.

BROWN RUFFLE SKELETON KEY SCARFLETTE

A twist on the choker from Chapter 2, this standout piece has steampunk written all over it. For best results, choose a variety of fabrics that have different colors and textures. You can leave the fabric edges raw, finish them with a zigzag stitch, or even hem them. Depending on the thickness of the fabric, a hem could create a stiff ruffle.

MATERIALS

- ❑ ¼ YD. (230MM) EACH OF 3 COORDINATING FABRICS

- ❑ ½ YD. (455MM) ¾–1" (20MM–25MM) LACE OR RIBBON

- ❑ 1 MEDIUM-SIZED SKELETON KEY

- ❑ CHAIN, PEARLS, AND CHARMS TO EMBELLISH

1 **Cut the fabric.** Cut the bottom fabric (closest to the skin) 5"–6" (125–150mm) long and the full width of the fabric. Cut the middle fabric approximately ¾"–1" (20–25mm) narrower than the bottom fabric, and the top fabric ¾"–1" (20–25mm) narrower than the middle fabric.

2 **Ruffle the fabric.** Ruffle each length of fabric down the center (see page 18). Once the fabric is ruffled, determine the circumference of your neck and add 2" (50mm) to create an overlap. Transfer that measurement to the ruffles and cut off the excess.

3 **Sew together the layers.** Layer the ruffled fabrics in the pre-determined order, matching the ruffling seams. Pin and sew through all the layers with a straight stitch.

4 **Sew on the lace trim.** Cut the ribbon or lace the same length as the scarflette. Pin in place on the top layer of fabric over the center seam. Stitch along each side of the ribbon or lace. This will help to keep it from folding over on itself. Fold under the raw edges of fabric and ribbon or lace to finish. Stitch.

5 **Add the skeleton key.** Hand stitch a skeleton key to one side of the scarflette so that the tooth extends beyond the edge. Cut a narrow piece of ribbon or fabric long enough to make a loop for the key's tooth. Line up the ribbon with the key's tooth and pin to the opposite edge of the scarflette. Stitch, turning under the edges.

Steampunk Your Wardrobe

Victorian Purse

No Victorian lady could be without her reticule, or purse, and I don't think you should be either. With so many choices of fabric, trim, and even shape, this is the perfect project to let your steampunk imagination run wild and achieve a custom look. Use the finished piece as a traditional change purse, a travel jewelry bag, or even a glasses case. Select a purse frame with a lot of filigree for a flowery Victorian look, or a plain metal frame for a more edgy steampunk vibe.

MATERIALS AND TOOLS

- ❏ METAL-HINGED PURSE FRAME

- ❏ STRONG GLUE OR EPOXY

- ❏ ½ YD. (455MM) DECORATIVE FABRIC FOR EXTERIOR OF PURSE

- ❏ ½ YD. (455MM) FABRIC FOR LINING

- ❏ ⅓ YD. (305MM) WIDE DECORATIVE BEADED TRIM

- ❏ ½ YD. (455MM) FRINGE TRIM (OPTIONAL)

- ❏ 1 YD. (1M) HEAVY CHAIN FOR THE SHOULDER STRAP (LESS IF ONLY MAKING A HANDLE)

- ❏ PAPER

- ❏ SCREWDRIVER

- ❏ PLIERS

1 **Draw the purse body shape.** Fold the paper in half and center the purse frame over the fold. Trace around the top and sides of the frame, then draw the body of the purse. A circular shape is shown, but any shape will work. On the template, mark the bottom of the hinges. Make the shape wider to give the purse more room.

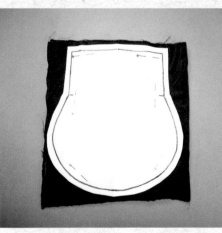

2 **Add the seam allowance.** Add a seam allowance by drawing a second line that makes the template ¼" (5mm) larger than the original tracing. Cut out.

3 **Cut the decorative and lining fabrics.** Fold the decorative fabric in half, right sides together. Pin the template to the fabric and cut out two pieces. Be sure to mark where the bottom of the hinge lies. Repeat with the lining fabric.

4 **Attach the ribbon.** Pin the decorative ribbon to the middle of the right sides of the purse body. Make sure the trim will meet at the bottom of the purse when the two sides are sewn together. Stitch along both sides of the ribbon.

5 **Sew on the fringe** If using fringe, pin the top edge of the trim to the edge of one piece of the decorative fabric, matching right sides. The fringe can go from hinge mark to hinge mark or to the very top of the purse, depending on the purse frame. Sew the fringe in place.

6 **Sew the purse pieces together.** Place the right sides of the purse body together and pin. Stitch the bottom, rounded portion of the fabric together between the hinge marks. Take care to only catch the top edge of the fringe trim in the seam.

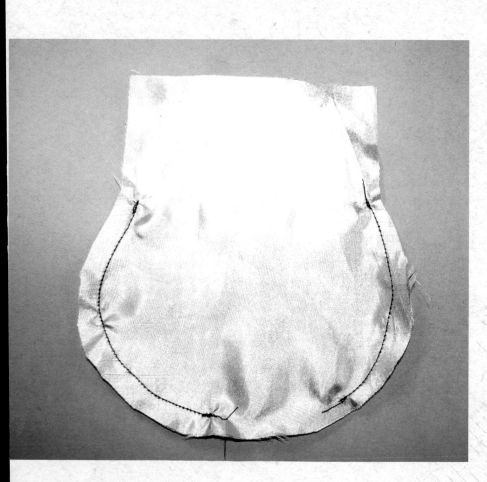

7 **Sew the lining.** Pin the lining together, matching right sides. Stitch the bottom portion between hinge marks, leaving a 2" (50mm) opening at the very bottom for turning.

8 **Sew the purse top together.** Without turning the pieces right side out, pin the fabric to the lining, matching right sides along the top and sides between the hinge marks. Stitch between the hinge marks.

9 **Turn the purse right side out.** Using the opening left in the bottom of the lining, gently turn the purse and lining right side out. Tuck in the raw edges and stitch the opening in the lining closed.

10 **Figure out what type of frame you have.** There are different frame styles and methods of attaching the purse to the frame. If there are holes along its edge, hand stitch the body of the purse to the frame. If it has a U-shaped channel, apply glue to the channel and wedge the fabric into the channel. The frame on the purse shown uses a two-piece frame.

11 **Attach the outer frame.** For the two-piece frame, hold the fabric up to the inner frame and mark the position of the holes. Glue the purse body to the frame, lining up the fabric with the hinges. Be careful to keep the glue out of the screw holes. It is easiest to glue one side, let the glue dry then glue the other side.

12 **Attach the frame.** Once the glue has set, use an awl, pin, or wooden skewer to punch through the fabric where the screw holes are located. Fit the inner frame in place and attach with the screws.

13 **Attach the chain.** Shorten the chain by opening a link and removing the excess chain. Attach to the purse by opening a link on each end or attaching jump rings. If desired, use a different material for the handle or twist together multiple lengths of chain for a more substantial strap/handle.

VICTORIAN LACE SHIRT

Lace and gauze can turn the plainest shirt into pure Victorian femininity. Use this technique to add some interest to any button-down shirt you have hanging in your closet. If you want to give the shirt an edgy look, try pairing it with some steampunk chain jewelry or a leather belt. You can also switch out the original buttons for some with filigree.

MATERIALS

- A FITTED BUTTON FRONT SHIRT

- 12" TO 16" (305MM—405MM) LIGHTWEIGHT, GAUZY FABRIC (CHEESECLOTH, LACE, OR CRUSHED BRIDAL TULLE)

- 2 FT. (610MM) 2" TO 3" (50MM—75MM)-WIDE GATHERED LACE

- 2 FT. (610MM) COORDINATING LACE TRIM

- MATCHING THREAD

- EMBELLISHMENTS (SUCH AS PEARLS, RIBBON, BOWS, ETC.)

1 **Remove any pockets.** If the shirt has patch pockets, use a seam ripper to remove them. If the shirt has a pocket on the inside that is accessible from a slit in the shirt, it may be unsuitable for this project.

2 **Cut the lightweight fabric.** Measure from the shoulder seam to the chest. Cut 2 pieces of the lightweight fabric 12–16" (305–405mm) wide and as long as the shoulder to chest measurement.

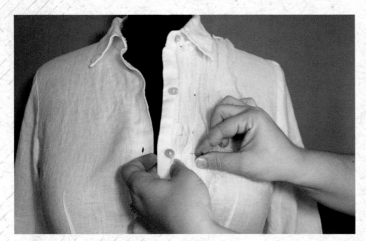

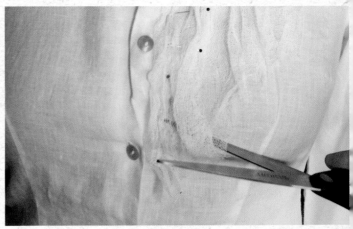

3 **Pin the fabric in place.** Use a pin to mark the point halfway between the arm seam and the base of the collar. Pin the lightweight fabric to both sides of the shirt front between the collar and the pin, tucking under raw edge at the top and gathering the fabric to fit. Do not extend the fabric beyond the shirt's buttons or buttonholes.

4 **Trim the excess and sew the fabric.** Trim any excess from the bottom edges of the fabric so it is even on both sides of the shirt. Stitch the fabric to the shirt along the edges using a small zigzag stitch.

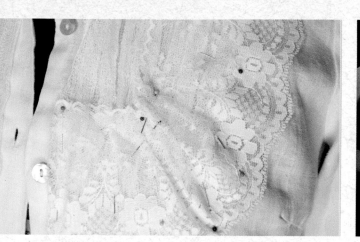

5 **Sew on the lace trim.** Pin the gathered edge of the lace trim to the outer edge of the lightweight fabric, making sure it covers the raw edge by 1" (25mm).Gather the inner corner of the lace so it lies flat as it goes around the corner. Repeat with the opposite side of the shirt, making sure both sides are even. Stitch.

6 **Remove the collar.** Cut the collar from the shirt, leaving approximately ½" (15mm) of the lower edge of the collar still attached. Turn the raw edge of the remaining collar under ½" (15mm) and stitch. If the collar will not be buttoned, remove the top button at the collar.

7 **Sew on the lace collar.** Pin the lace trim to the collar so the edge of the trim rides above the collar band. Extend the trim to the button and buttonhole at the edges of the collar if the button was removed. Turn raw edges under and stitch. Apply additional trim to the cuffs, stopping at the button and edge of the buttonhole.

8 **Add embellishments.** Embellish as desired with pearls, bows, and ribbon.

LEATHER WAIST CINCHER

This piece is a true eye-catcher! Whether you pair it with a casual shirt or a cocktail dress, it gives off just the right steampunk vibe. Give your cincher a custom look and fit by making small changes to the design during the drafting process.

Just visible behind model Sierra Gitlin is a 1907 Orient Runabout, produced by the Waltham Manufacturing Company. Modeled after the earlier horse-drawn buckboard, this open two-seater contained a rear-mounted, air-cooled, V-twin engine; leaf springs; continuously-variable friction transmission; and dual chain drive. Due to its wooden frame and body, the car was extremely lightweight. The vehicle was controlled by a hand lever shifter, left pedal rear brake, right pedal "clutch," and a throttle and ignition advance/retard located atop the steering wheel.

MATERIALS AND TOOLS

- LIGHTWEIGHT LEATHER APPROXIMATELY 8" (205MM) WIDE AND THE LENGTH OF YOUR WAIST CIRCUMFERENCE. NOTE: WAIST CINCHERS ARE TYPICALLY SMALLER THAN THE ACTUAL WAIST MEASUREMENT. IF YOU DO NOT WANT TO WEAR THIS CINCHED, CHOOSE A PIECE OF LEATHER 4" (100MM) LONGER THAN YOUR WAIST CIRCUMFERENCE.

- A SHEET OF PAPER APPROXIMATELY 10" (255MM) BY THE CIRCUMFERENCE OF YOUR WAIST. NOTE: WRAPPING PAPER, WAXED PAPER, OR FREEZER PAPER ARE GOOD OPTIONS.

- 3 LARGE SWING BAG CLASPS (WITH RIVETS)

- SMALL- TO MEDIUM-SIZED GROMMETS

- RIVETS

- ADDITIONAL RIVETS AND GEARS FOR EMBELLISHMENT (OPTIONAL)

- SHARP SCISSORS OR CRAFT KNIFE

- SMALL HEAVY-DUTY CLIPS

- HAMMER

- RULER

- LEATHER HOLE PUNCH

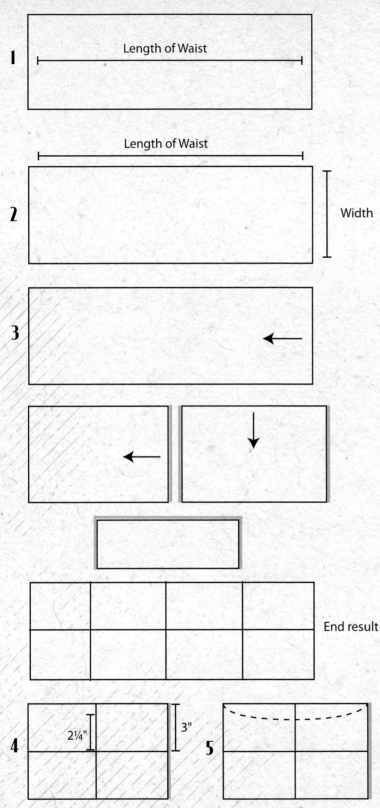

1. **Measure your waist.** Measure your waist across the belly button. If you plan to wear this cinched, cut the paper the length of your waist measurement. If you do not want to cinch it, cut the paper 4" (100mm) longer than your waist measurement.

2. **Cut paper to width.** The waist cincher should start at the sternum and continue to just below the belly button. For most people, this is approximately 7½" (190mm). If a wider or narrower cincher is desired, make any necessary adjustments to this measurement then transfer it to the paper. Cut the paper to this width, creating a long rectangle.

3. **Fold the paper.** Fold the paper in half, meeting the two short sides, and then in half again. These folds will mark the center front and the two areas on the cincher that will fall just over your hip bones. Unfold both folds then fold the paper in half again, this time lengthwise. Be sure to crease the paper along all folds.

4. **Mark more measurements on the pattern.** Unfold the paper and refold once so that the two short ends meet. There should be two creases that intersect in the center of the paper. On the short crease, make a mark 2¼" (57mm) inches away from the long center fold. On the folded edge, make a mark 3" (126mm) away from the long center fold.

5. **Connect the marks.** Connect the top unfolded corner point and the marks using a gentle curve. Cut out along the line.

6

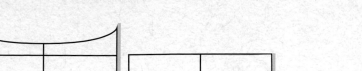

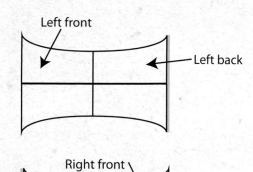

Left front

Left back

7

Right front

Right back

6 **Cut the bottom curve.** Leaving the paper folded with short edges together, re-fold the paper along the center length. Using the curved edge as a guide, trace the curve on the opposite side of the paper and cut out.

7 **Labeling the pattern.** Mark the cut end "left front" and the folded end "left back." Turn the paper over and mark the cut end on that side "right front" and the folded end "right back." This will help ensure proper placement on the leather.

9 **Mark the rivet hole positions.** Fold back ¾"–1" (20–25mm) along the long vertical straight edge of both front pieces and hold in place with clips if necessary. Lay the two folded edges together and evenly space the swing clasps on the leather. Using the clasps as a guideline, mark the position of the rivet holes.

8 **Cut the template.** Cut the template along the three short folds, creating four pattern pieces. Place the template pieces on the underside of the leather and outline. Cut out the pieces using kitchen shears or a razor tipped craft knife.

10 **Punch the rivet holes.** Punch through both layers of leather at the rivet hole marks.

11 **Attach the swing clasps.** Attach the swing clasps with the rivets by hammering the rivets in place. Protect the rivet from damage by placing a scrap piece of cloth or leather between the rivet and the hammer.

12 **Trim the extra leather flaps.** Trim the extra leather that shows where the leather was folded back.

13 **Punch the back grommets on one side.** Place the grommets close together along the long vertical straight edge of one back piece. The number used will depend upon the size of the grommets. It is important to keep the grommets close together to avoid puckering when the cincher is pulled tight. Mark the placement of each grommet and punch through the leather at each mark.

14 **Punch the back grommets on the other side.** Place the back piece with the holes on top of the other back piece, matching right sides. Use the holes in the top piece to mark where the holes in the second piece should be. This will help ensure they will line up evenly when the cincher is complete. Punch through the leather at each mark.

15 **Set the grommets.** Push the front piece of the grommet through the leather, and line up with the rear grommet. Set the grommets with a hammer and the grommet set or with a grommet tool. Be sure the grommets are tightly secured so they do not come loose when in use.

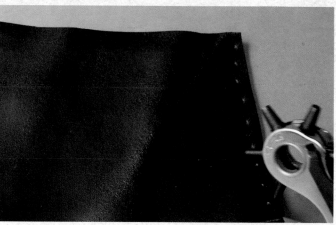

16 Mark the side rivet locations.
Place the short, straight edge of one front piece over the short, straight edge of the corresponding back piece. Overlap the edges approximately ½" (15mm), with the wrong side of the front situated on top of the right side of the back piece. Space the rivets evenly along the overlap and mark where the holes should be.

17 Punch the side rivet holes.
Use the leather hole punch to make holes at the marks. Place the front and back pieces together, matching the short straight edges. Using the first piece as a guide, mark the holes in the back piece and punch. Repeat with the remaining two pieces, using the first piece as a guide.

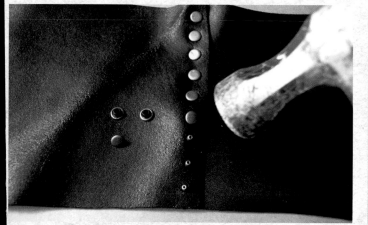

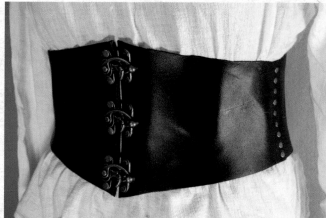

18 Attach the rivets.
Lay the left back piece, right side up, on a flat surface and place the wrong side of the left front piece on top, matching holes. Attach the two pieces with rivets. Repeat with the right side pieces, making sure to put the front piece over top of the back piece.

19 Thread up the back.
To wear, thread a ribbon through the grommets in the back pieces and tie. If desired, embellish with additional rivets and gears.

Brown Capelet

Breathe new life into an old coat with some simple alterations and additions. The design hints at a Victorian cape with some steampunk-inspired closures and hardware. You can push the envelope by adding extra closures or give the piece a more traditional look by replacing the clasps and rings with buttons. Don't forget that a piece of chain makes a great accent on a piece of steampunk clothing.

MATERIALS

- ❑ Rounded shoulder coat
- ❑ Double wide bias tape
- ❑ Matching thread
- ❑ 2 metal clasps
- ❑ 2 D-rings
- ❑ Approximately a 6" x 6" (150 x 150mm) square of lightweight leather
- ❑ Fabric pencil or marker

1 **Select a coat.** Choose a coat with rounded shoulders in a slightly larger size than you would normally wear.

2 **Determine the length.** Determine the length of the capelet by measuring from the shoulder seam down the front of the coat. It is best to not go past the bottom of the armhole. The back can be the same length or longer than the front.

3 **Mark the length.** Use a tape measure and pins to transfer the measurement determined in step 2 to the front and back of the coat. Use a fabric pencil or marker to connect the marks and extend a straight line over to the sleeves.

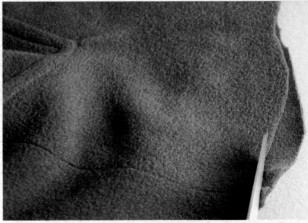

4 **Cut the coat to length.** Cut along the line, cutting through both the coat and the lining. If the sleeve is still connected at the underarm, cut it along the seam. Trim any uneven edges, especially around the sleeves. Trim the lining so it is approximately 2" (50mm) shorter than the capelet.

5 **Trim away uneveness along the bottom.** Fold the capelet in half along the center back seam, bringing the sleeve seams together. Trim away any unevenness so that both sides of the capelet are even.

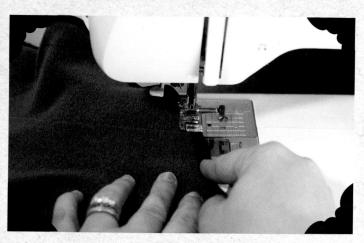

6 **Keep the edges from fraying.** Cover the raw edge of the bottom of the capelet with a coordinating wide double-fold bias tape. Zigzag over the raw edge of the lining to prevent fraying.

7 **Cut leather strips.** Cut two strips of leather for each clasp and D-ring. Cut the strips long enough to cover the buttonholes and as wide as the openings on the clasps and rings. Remove the buttons. Slip a leather strip through each clasp and position over the button holes. Slip a leather strip through each D-ring and position where the buttons were attached.

8 **Attach the clasps and D-rings.** Attach the clasps and D-rings to the capelet by sewing through the leather around the edges and along each side of the clasps and D-rings.

9 **Add extra fasteners.** Attach additional clasps and D-ring closures to the front of the capelet, if desired. The capelet also can be fastened with buttons, utilizing existing buttonholes, or with ribbon ties.

PLUM SHIRT

For this last project, I combine most of the skills you've already learned to make this plum steampunk shirt. The shirt features tulle, ruffles, cabbage roses, and trim in another fabric. You have the option of gathering it at the back for additional flair. As with any of the previous projects, alter the design as you desire by adding embellishments or using a different color of fabric.

MATERIALS

- ❑ 1 BUTTON-FRONT DRESS SHIRT

- ❑ 2–3 YD. (2–2¾M) COORDINATING FABRIC (LIKE VELVET) TO BE USED AT NECK, SLEEVES, AND HEM

- ❑ 1½ YD. (1⅜M) SHEER COORDINATING FABRIC (LIKE TULLE) TO BE USED AT THE NECK

- ❑ 1½ YD. (1⅜M) COORDINATING LACE, APPROXIMATELY 3" TO 4"(75MM–100MM) WIDE, TO BE USED AT THE NECK

- ❑ BUTTONS

- ❑ 5"(125MM) RIBBON, APPROXIMATELY 2" (50MM) WIDE

- ❑ 2 YD. (2M) TULLE FOR A BUSTLE (OPTIONAL)

- ❑ EMBELLISHMENTS

1 **Choose a shirt.** Choose a loose or slightly fitted shirt with no upper pockets. A larger shirt can be gathered in the back.

2 **Create the V-neck.** Cut away the collar following the natural fold of the garment, creating a V-neck.

3 **Cut the bottom edge of the shirt.** Cut the fabric at a downward angle beginning at the center front near the natural waist. Cut across the front and around the sides, creating a gentle curve that continues down to approximately 6" (150mm) past the side seam, then curves around to a line straight across to the center back. Ensure both sides are even.

4 **Add darts.** If desired, add darts to the front or take in the sides. Leave extra room in the back for gathering.

5 **Choose the ruffle fabric.** When choosing fabric for making the ruffles, remember that different textures and weights will add interest. Depending on the desired look, hem or zigzag the fabric prior to ruffling. Another option is to cut the ruffle fabric twice the desired depth of the ruffle plus 1" (25mm), fold it so the long sides meet, wrong sides together, and stitch down the raw edges. This method allows the right side of the fabric to be visible from both the top and bottom sides of the ruffle.

6 **Decide on ruffle gathering options.** The fabric for the ruffles can be gathered as it is sewn onto the garment or gathered separately, then attached. If multiple ruffles are desired, it is easier to gather the fabric before attaching it to the garment. It also is possible to use both methods on the same garment. Regardless of the method, be aware that it may be necessary to sew multiple pieces of fabric together before gathering to create a long enough ruffle. Refer to page 18 for more information on creating ruffles.

7 **Taper the collar ruffle fabric.** Taper the ends of the collar ruffle fabric so the ruffle decreases in height as it approaches the center front seam and the button closure.

8 **Sew on the collar ruffle.** Pin the collar ruffle to the neckline, matching the raw edges. Stitch.

9 **Stitch the neckline seam allowance.** Turn the raw edges to the inside of the shirt, bringing the ruffle up so it sits along the edge of the neckline. On the right side of the fabric, stitch the seam allowance to the shirt to keep it in place.

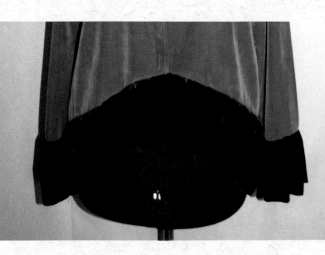

10 **Add additional neck ruffles.** Layer additional ruffles along the neckline, if desired. For best results, choose lightweight fabrics and gather the ruffles down the center of the fabric rather than at the edge. Pin the additional ruffles to the shirt, matching the gathering of the ruffle and the stitching applied to the shirt in Step 8.

11 **Cut the sleeves.** Cut the sleeves so they fall at or just above the wrist. They will be finished with a ruffle, so take this into account when determining the length.

12 **Attach the sleeve and bottom ruffles.** Cut the ruffle fabric into a long strip that is as wide as the desired depth of the ruffle plus ¾" (20mm) if the ruffle is to be hemmed, double the depth plus 1" (25mm) if the ruffle is to be doubled. It may be necessary to stitch two or more strips of fabric together to make a ruffle long enough for the bottom edge of the shirt. Finish the edge of the ruffle as desired by hemming or doubling as described in Step 6. Attach the ruffle to the bottom of the shirt and also to the sleeves, using the method described in Steps 8 and 9.

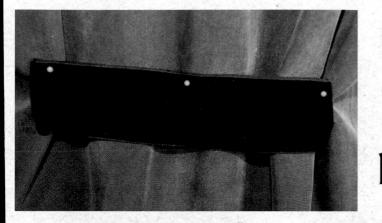

13 **Hem the back gather ribbon.** Hem the raw edges of the ribbon. Bring the short edges of the ribbon together and mark the center with a pin. Find the center back of the shirt by bringing the side seams together. Mark with a pin near the waistline.

14 **Attach the ribbon.** Pin the ribbon to the shirt back, matching centers. Pin the edges of the ribbon to the shirt back, creating a gather under the ribbon. The amount of fabric gathered depends upon the shirt size and how much extra fabric is available. Stitch the short ends of the ribbon to the shirt.

15 **Attach the bustle.** To add a bustle, fold the tulle in half, placing the fold off center. Fold it in half a second time, again placing the fold off center. Gather the tulle approximately 10" (254mm) from the fold. Attach the gathered edge to the wide ribbon in back, placing the folded edge on top. If desired, add flowers or other embellishments.

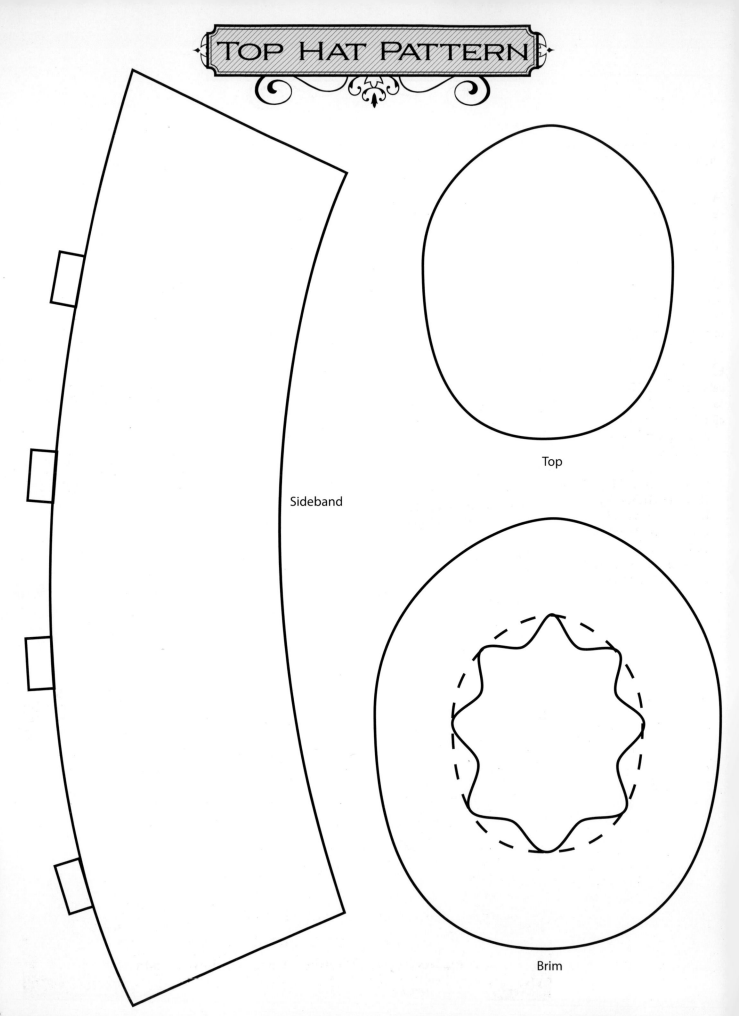

Top

Sideband

Brim

INDEX

Acquisition editor: Peg Couch

Assistant editor: Katie Weeber

Copy editor: Paul Hambke

Cover and layout designer: Ashley Millhouse

Cover and gallery photographer: Scott Kriner

Developmental editor: Lisa Caylor

Editor: Kerri Landis

Indexer: Jay Kreider

Model: Sierra Gitlin

Proofreader: Lynda Jo Runkle

Step-by-step and model photographer: Calista Taylor

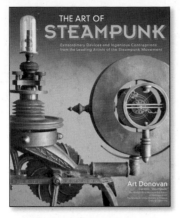

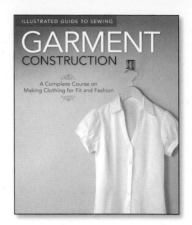
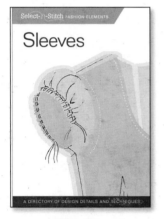

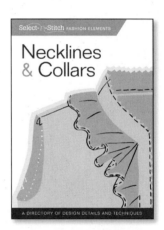

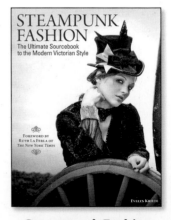